One Minute Wisdom

Simple, Effective and Tested Tips for Sustainable Growth

Sanjay Sarda

 pencil

ISBN 978-93-5458-242-4
© Sanjay Sarda 2021
Published in India 2021 by Pencil

A brand of
One Point Six Technologies Pvt. Ltd.
123, Building J2, Shram Seva Premises,
Wadala Truck Terminal, Wadala (E)
Mumbai 400037, Maharashtra, INDIA
E connect@thepencilapp.com
W www.thepencilapp.com

DISCLAIMER: *The opinions expressed in this book are those of the authors and do not purport to reflect the views of the Publisher.*

Author biography

Sanjay Sarda is alumni of IIT Kharagpur and IIM Ahmedabad with over 27 years of working experience in India and USA, which includes multiple entrepreneurial stints and diverse consulting responsibilities. He is a Certified Corporate Director by IICA and IOD and one of the first few individuals in India to qualify to be an Independent Director. He is also serving diverse set of businesses and HNIs in the capacity of virtual CEO, helping them in providing solutions for critical challenges, decision making and business strategy.

Earlier, he was associated with many multinationals like, Monsanto, Procter and Gamble, General Electric, Tata Consultancy Services, IBM Global Services, CSX Corporation, Krishidhan Group, and Ernst and Young LLP, in diverse roles.

On social fronts, he is actively associated in leadership roles with Rotary International and Saturday Club Global Trust.

CONTENTS

Foreword

I met Sanjay couple of years ago in a club meeting, and since then we are friends. He is a person known for his wisdom, analytical power and giving unbiased solutions. He is ready to help his friends and relatives by giving his opinion on any challenges of their lives. We spend hours and days together and discuss life.

'One Minute Wisdom' is real life wisdom of Sanjay as a self-made man, he taking charge of his life when he was a school going kid and has huge experience, ups & downs in life from USA to Akola, from jobs in various prestigious organizations to owning multiple factories to a business strategy consultant to an angel investor, and many more things. He summarized his life learnings in this book called 'One Minute Wisdom'.

Sanjay shares his 'One Minute wisdom' topic before publishing on his WhatsApp group and in our fortnightly dinner meetings. And after discussion he fine tunes it and then publish, making sure no stone left unturned.

You are holding a treasure in your hand & this treasure of wisdom will transform your life forever.

Dr. Manish Sethi Jain

Co-founder of Abundance Innovative Education, Motivational Speaker, Author and Leadership Forum Leader.

Preface

As the name suggests; it will not take more than one minutes to read one chapter in this book. There are 52 such chapters talking about action items to address challenges related to day do day working life of entrepreneur, businessperson or working professional.

During my active professional career of over 27 years, I was fortunate to get opportunity to work with diverse set of industries in India an USA. And prior to that, time spent at IIT Kharagpur contributed a lot to my approach in providing solutions.

I was sharing such tips as and where required for many years and recently thought about communicating one tip every week by social media. After consistently sharing one message every Monday for last one year; now thought about compiling all these 52 wisdom tips in book format.

As a reader; you may start with any chapter randomly as per your choice and interest. I suggest to keep this book on your working desk and quickly check one tip during coffee time occasionally. I am sure you will be able co-relate these tips to your pressing issues and find easy and implementable solutions. Sincere best wishes for your sustainable growth.

Acknowledgements

At the outset, I would like to acknowledge and sincerely thank my parents for giving me total freedom since childhood, whether it is for selection of school, college, curriculum or work. Their unconditional support and zero interference in my decisions helped me develop learning and experimental mindset, which helped in creating value for many organizations.

I was fortunate to get many good partners and associates throughout my working career, which helped me in learning and creation of these wisdom tips for real life circumstances. I am grateful to all my associates for encouragement in implementing new ideas and thoughts.

I would like to especially mention my gratitude for Mr. Sushil Karwa, Group Managing Director at Krishidhan, who entrusted me for various critical, challenging and seemingly impossible roles and responsibilities. I was able to test many of these tips mentioned in the book during my active association with Krishidhan.

I thank all my current business associates, family and friends for listening and implementing these tips in their day to day working; which is a great source of energy and encouragement for me.
Thank you.

Pay more than what an employee deserves

During salary negotiations, ensure that the final agreed payment is slightly higher than what is deserved by the employee. This small increment over and above the benchmark set by the self esteem of the employee will push the person to his/her limits to deliver more value.

On the contrary, if payment is even slightly less than this benchmark figure, it will have significant adverse impact on performance.

Off course; it does not mean that you pay irrationally higher amount. The trick is; structure your discussions in such a way to help the person realize his/her real value or real worth; and then make your final offer.

This applies to both the situations; at the time of hiring and performance appraisal.

Use only company owned mobile number for business

For every employee, who interacts with anyone outside the office, including vendors, customers and associates; should use company owned sim cards only. This will help in positive brand management by standardizing one important touch point. Additionally, it will ensure very smooth transition whenever a person leaves job.

Just imagine, your top salesperson leaves and join your competition; whenever a customer call on his/her number, it will be absolutely natural outcome that product or services of your competitor will be sold to your loyal customer.

Sometimes, losses due to such unintentional cross connects can cause major damage to the business.

So; if you are not already practicing this; it's time to act today.

Success and growth of your business depends on how quickly you hire professionals

Professionally qualified team is one of the proven driving factor for business growth.

Prima-facie, these candidates are relatively expensive and many times, we pull on with relatively less qualified team for some quick savings. However, time lost with this approach can prove to be very expensive in medium to long term.

It is advisable to continuously review the team structure and personal attributes of each member and replace bottom 10% with highly qualified professionals in respective domains.

With this approach, you will be surprised to see how quick the business shifts to fast track.

Take a pause before picking up a phone call

Many times, as our phone rings, we immediately pick up the call. At that time, our mind might be occupied with something else, or may be going through some extreme emotions. And all this will have impact on the outcome of this upcoming telephonic conversation.

It is better to take a pause before picking up any incoming call. Initially this pause can be some 8-10 seconds which can be reduced with practice to faction of second for sure.

During this pause you need to first come out of your current mindset and thought process and then think about the calling person with any connecting references or pending issues. Also think about any greetings or wishes specific to the person, festival or time of the day. Also use this pause to bring back smile on your face before picking the call

This practice will certainly make your every conversation a pleasant one and most importantly, the outcome will be in your favor.

Review written communication before sending

As you know shelf life of a written communication is longer and many times it is permanent.

Whether you write message on WhatsApp, SMS, email or any other platform; before hitting send button it is a very good practice to review it once. If it is about proposals, agreements or more important communication; take a pause of few hours or one day before review and then send.

In addition to fixing miscellaneous errors like spelling and grammar; many times it will avoid major miscommunication or misunderstandings. Sometimes people even do not reply to such unintentional errors and we do not get opportunity to correct and we keep wondering what happened.

If you start practicing this for few days; you will notice how many times you change your message which otherwise would have gone in it's undesired language and tone.

Build technology fund for safeguarding future of business

We all agree that technology is one of the major growth driver for any business. Also we know that speed of change in technology is increasing every day. Also cost of new technology in the initial phase is significantly high and then it drops after some time.

Most of the businesses face challenge with budget allocation for technology due to unreasonably higher cost of technology in the initial phase. At the same time, it is important to adopt it as quick as possible to stay ahead in competition.

The only solution is, reserve some reasonable share from profits in separate technology fund; so that over next couple of years this fund will give you the competitive edge by quickly acquiring new technologies which will drive further growth.

Finance and Accounts are two separate functions

Many times, especially a small business owner mix finance and accounts functions together; which is not correct and not beneficial for business in long run since it leads to ignorance of core finance functions.

Basically accounting refers to recording day-to-day flow of money and preparing financial reports. While finance is a broader function dealing with management of assets and liabilities and planning for the future.

In other words, accounts can be treated as small sub-function of finance. Accounting is more about accurate reporting of what has already happened and compliance with relevant laws and standards. While finance is more about analysing these reports for decision making with reference to protecting and enhancing wealth.

Friends, as a business owner; your focus should be more on finance.

Develop culture of negative reporting

Especially at the management or higher levels, develop a culture of negative reporting.

Usually, we collect lot of information and data from our team, which definitely helps in analysis, planning, taking appropriate actions and further strategy fine-tuning.

However, reading such reports on regular basis is time consuming activity; and as a result either important points are overlooked or even sometimes reports itself are ignored.

Instead, design a report in such a way that only deviation from planned or desired outcome are reported. With this type of report, content for the management will reduce significantly and they have to look at problem areas only. Desired final outcome of such reporting is an extremely short report with just one word "Nil".

Just imaging kind of efficiency which will be brought in the system with the culture of negative reporting.

Attend conferences and trade shows regularly

As we must have experienced, speed of change is increasing every day. With this, sometimes even the perfectly working business model or products or services gets outdated before it is noticed by many of us.

Relevant trade shows and conferences can play a very important role in preparing the business for upcoming change. It is a very good practice to regularly attend such event as part of investment in business.

Also choose the events, so as to get exposure of at least one step higher than your current state of business. Wherever possible, visit international events and some trending technology events which may not be directly connected to your existing operations.

If you develop this culture in the organization where all team leaders are getting such exposure; you will certainly notice visible positive change in the organization.

Know valuation of your business

Do you know market value of your business today? If you wish to sell full or part of your business, at what price you will sell? Or at what price you can find a buyer? Or, if you have to start a fresh; at what price you will pay for acquiring exactly similar business?

There are two basic ways business can make money. One is by selling products and/or services. And Second is by way of increasing valuation of business, which is the primary factor of wealth creation in most cases.

If you do not know valuation of your business now and if you do not keep reviewing it at regular intervals; you will never know that if you are putting efforts in the right business or not. Also, you will never notice impact of external factors before it is too late to correct.

With change in mindset to earning money by valuation route; you will automatically stay focused on continuous growth and accept the change and external impact at early stage to convert it in your favor.

Never deduct salary as punishment

Especially in small and medium size businesses, it is noticed that deduction of amount from salary for any mistake is very common. Sometimes it is for coming late or going early or making some mistake due to which company lose some money and many such small reasons.

As a business owner; we need to distinguish between loss due to some error while performing duties and loss due gross negligence or bad intentions. We need to have clear guidelines with reference to integrity and negligence. If these guidelines are violated; you can seriously consider firing the employee; however if it is within the set limits; it should be absorbed as operating loss.

If employee is genuine and loss is not intentional; any deduction will have long lasting negative impact. In such case net looser will be the business and not the employee.

So next time before you think about deduction of salary; take a decision either to fire the employee or absorb the loss.

Make payment on time, but **NOT** before due date

We all agree that making payments on time is good for the business in many ways. However; there are some businesses, for the reasons like, coming in good books of vendors, availability of positive cash flow, or sometimes just for no reason make payments few days before due date.

There are two major losses to the business in short as well as long term with this so called positive gesture.

First of all; believe that the finance cost based on due date or agreed credit period is built in the price of goods and services. So by making payments earlier; you are directly losing on this amount; which will be significant over the period of time.

Another major loss is long term. Once you start making payments earlier; people take it for granted and start expecting it every time. And many vendors leverage this assumption and make other commitments in their business based on this. So whenever you fail to meet this extra favor of early payment; people may face difficulties; which will have direct impact on your business relationship.

On the contrary; if you stick to the due date, your money and goodwill both will rise with time.

Prepare List of Activities which can be Delegated

As a business owner or senior executive, we do many things in the business. To grow further, it is a proven fact that we need to create leaders to follow us. Challenge is; where to begin?

You can start with preparing list of activities or tasks which you do not like to do, or where you do not have sufficient knowledge or expertise to deliver best results.
Also identify things for which you will not have time to do, if your business size is doubled from current level.

Start working on developing leaders and team members to take care of these activities, so that you can move ahead with activities of higher value.

It is not a one time action; but needs to be done at regular frequency, say every three months to maintain the pace of growth.

Never talk to L-2 employees

There are multiple layers of employees in the organization. Usually we hire manager who reports to the owner and gets the work done from the executives in his/her team.

Many times the owner directly talks to the executive for getting reports or giving instructions. If the executive is good and genuine it will create confusion for him/her about whom to listen and how to balance between Manager and Owner. On the other hand, if the executive is not committed or engaged with the business, it gives a clear excuse for not doing work and can easily manipulate both Owner and Manager. With time, even the good manager also stops working since he/she knows that the Owner will anyways get the work done from the executive directly. In long run, it acts as a major hurdle in organization's growth.

So communication should be routed through the manager only. This will reduce owner's work while delivering significant improvement in results.

(Note: L-2 means anyone who is reporting to the manager who is directly reporting to you)

Document every important communication

Mostly, business relationships are adversely affected due to gap in understanding. Significant part of our communication happens verbally. Interpretations may differ depending on language, words, tone, mindset, mood and presumptions; which creates a problem at later stage.

Sometimes, it could mean major people or financial loss to the organization. To avoid all such issues; it is best to follow practice of documentation for every communication, whether it is with your employee, customer, vendor, partner or any other associate.

Wherever possible, ask for written confirmation about the discussion with key measurable action items from the other party. If it is not possible, you can initiate communication by sending discussion note by written message.

In addition to avoiding confusion and related losses; it will improve the productivity and positive outcome due to clarity and documented action items.

Clearly define exit clause for successful long term association

Mostly, all associations whether it is a partnership, joint venture, employment or any other long-term relationship begins on very positive note with everything looking good with well aligned goals and objectives of all parties.

With time, even for genuine reasons; life goals and vision may deviate. In such situations, if exit is not clearly defined; it is a human tendency or sometimes compulsion to pull on. Such less committed efforts by one party is detrimental to the association or organization in long term.

If exit clause is clearly defined, it protect the interest of both exiting and continuing party in future. And mostly every time it proves to be a win-win situation.

Additional most important benefit is; since people know they can exit anytime; they don't give up for small and temporary issues and continue to put best efforts. Once these short spells of disengagement are over, the association continues to grow to next level.

Give royal welcome to new employee

Growth of any organization is directly linked to commitment and engagement level of it's employees. From employee's point of view, quality of engagement depends on culture and image of the organization which is linked to the perceptions. First impression plays a vital role in building these perceptions.

We spend lots of time and resources in recruiting a good employee. But many times, after joining we start expecting results or output from day one; which sometimes make things difficult in long run.

For any new person joining the organization; there will be some level of anxiety and discomfort in the initial period. If we design this time to make it a royal welcome for this new person; it will be remembered for long time, resulting in positive outcome for the organization.

If this welcome experience is positively strong; it automatically takes care of small discomforts during day to day working in future.

Subject of written communication decides the outcome

Whenever we initiate some written communication, first thing which sets the tone of discussion is the "Subject".

Subject is something which decides whether your message is accepted or ignored. If not ignored, then it decides what will be the priority of your message.

Additionally; it can also set the mood of recipient which can potentially change the outcome. And if the subject is successful in setting the mood of recipient the way we want it; the outcome will also be favourable.

It is applicable to all modes of communication. If provision of mentioning subject is not available; similar outcome can be achieved by first sentence or paragraph of the message.

When a succession plan is needed; it's too late to start

Many businesses think about succession when there is vacancy.

Any vacancy will follow challenging time of different intensities depending on position and culture of the organization. Mostly, teams shift to fire fighting mode after any sudden gap created due to the vacancy leaving no time for planning.

Succession does not mean appointment of someone just to fill the gap; but keep someone ready to fill any anticipated or sudden gap in future. Succession planning is a very rigorous and ongoing process applicable to almost all critical positions in the organization.

Working on succession plan at the right time, when it is not needed; can define the future trajectory of business growth by safeguarding it whenever needed. It also facilitates smooth transition of responsibilities in normal course of business.

Be aware of hidden audience

There are two primary set of audience when we communicate; one is someone with whom we directly interact and other is the real audience which is mostly hidden.

For example, when we talk to media person; we are actually connecting with the audience linked to this media person. Also when we write the letter or business proposal; although it is addressed to someone with whom we interact; but the decision maker could be different.

All our communication, words used, tone, language, etc. should be selected with the hidden audience in mind and not only the person with whom we directly interact.

With clear understating of our objective, our desired results and with regular practice; art of identification of hidden audience can be mastered; leading to higher success rate of our communication.

Know lifetime value of your customer

Every customer has clearly measurable life time value. It can be different for every business depending on type of product or service, industry, size, mode of operation, etc.

Once we know life time value of a customer; efforts can be targeted for customer acquisition with clear focus. It also helps in allocation of appropriate marketing budget for customer acquisition.

For example, if first transaction value of your product is Rs. 100 but average lifetime value of a customer is Rs. 500; you can even offer your first product for free and still make profit of Rs. 400. However; in this example, if lifetime value is not taken into consideration, all marketing activities tend to be designed around profit from first transaction only; which may not be sufficient to achieve growth in medium to long term.

Working on business plan focused around life time value of customer can open up significant upside potential for growth. At the same time not doing so; can keep the business in long term struggle mode.

Be a dream employer for your next generation

Most family business owners are worried about whether their next generation will join the family business or not?

Whenever the young generation is ready to start working after completing education; it will be natural for them to compare the business with other opportunities available in the market.

If your business is ready to offer better opportunity as compared with the existing other options, then only, you can attract this new generation to join the family business.

Some of the thing you can do to begin your journey of branding as dream employer is work on long term growth plans, have defined organization and reporting structure, have clearly defined remuneration package for working family members, have pleasant and appropriately luxurious work space, have professional team members to head core business functions and have expert advisors on board who can act as mentor.

Work as employee and enjoy wealth as owner

In most family owned businesses; the promotor, majority shareholder and managing director are same. Many times, it acts as hurdle in decision making due to emotional connect and conflicting business interests.

Wherever possible, owner and management can be separated. But if not; one can develop the habit of working as CEO and not as shareholder or owner.

One simple tip is; even though you are the sole responsible person; start working as CEO or Managing Director who has to report to the Board and whose job and remuneration depends on performance.

With this, you will start delivering best results as CEO or Managing Director creating more value for all the stakeholders. Also, at the end of the year; major beneficiary is only you as a shareholder with increase in wealth.

Reconfirm receipt of important messages

Many times, in day to day work we send some message and assure ourselves or assume that action will be taken.

There are fairly good chances that the message might not have been received by the recipient. Even tough with some tools, we get automatic read receipts; there are many genuine reasons when these read receipts are not accurate. Also, some times the message is received but not understood as desired.

So, if the communication and desired action is important; it is always better to get a clear confirmation from the recipient before assuming that it is received.

As a simple example, imagine that you sent message to your driver for picking you up from the airport, late hours in the evening; and keep waiting since nobody turns up for pick-up.

This practice becomes more relevant if communication is not happening in-person and if required actions are pre-requisites for something else.

When holding position of authority; request instead of telling

While delegating any task, we have two choices; either to tell the person to do it or request the person to do it. Even one step forward, we can ask the person if he/she will do the work.

Since you are in the position of authority; answer to your question can not be negative. So, regardless of how you communicate, you will get what you want. Then why not chose the option which gives better results.

Major difference here is; when task is told, although it may be part of routine work, it will be taken as order with lesser engagement levels. But, when it is asked for; and the person replies affirmatively; it becomes own task and naturally executed with higher engagement levels.

Try this in real life for few days; and see the difference in results for yourself.

Develop habit of ZERO unread messages

We use emails, WhatsApp and other messaging tools for our day to day functions in business. Messages in our inbox can be broadly classified as important and not so important. If we assume that since it is received by us, it is important; then there is no choice but to read it in timely manner. If not, see to it that you don't receive unwanted messages.

Especially, when it comes to business; there has to be a time in a day or multiple times in a day depending on nature of business; you should have ZERO unread messages.

This will certainly improve the productivity in short term and help in building stronger brand image in long term.

Just in case, if you have noticed; successful and big people will reply very quickly to all communication, which is possible only when messages are read promptly.

Start taking time-off, especially when your presence is required the most

As you know; to grow a business, team is needed. And the leader or business owner needs to delegate important functions to the manager. To adapt the culture of delegation is sometimes the most difficult task, especially in the beginning.

This is one effective trick which helps in shifting to delegation mode quickly with comfort. Take some time off, especially when your presence is required the most. It can be couple of hours, one fully day, couple of days or more depending on type of activities and your role. And then slowly increase the duration and frequency of time-off.

When the boss is not available the subordinate usually quickly accepts the responsibility and act with authority. With some repetitions it becomes the habit and easy for you to delegate and comfortable for the team members to deliver.

Additionally, it can be a planned exercise to minimize any damage due to your absence.

Differentiate between Rules and Guidelines

In every organization or working environment, we have set of principles and policies which we expect everyone to follow. Broadly, all policies can be categorized as either Rules or Guidelines.

It is observed that many times there is a fine line between rules and guidelines which is used by the defaulter as excuse. To avoid this, need to clearly differentiate between Rules and Guidelines.

Rules are something where a clear and measurable action and/or punishment is defined in case these are violated; with violations clearly measurable by any party. Guidelines are something which are expected or desired things to be done. There can be incentive to follow guidelines but no punishment for violation.

With clear demarcation of Rules and Guidelines; you will certainly notice better discipline, higher engagement levels and improvement in performance at large.

Respect lunch and tea breaks

We do give lunch and tea breaks to all our employees. In most organizations, time of break is also fixed. But it is observed that breaks are not followed all the time. Especially if the owner/boss is having some different schedule; others are forced to delay these breaks. Sometimes, for ongoing meetings and urgent tasks we tend to skip or delay these breaks.

Any deviation on break timings will have direct impact on performance of the team. With habit, or as indicated by biological clock, the person's mind is expecting a break. Any delay will impact in loss of focus, which leads to adverse impact on performance.

Occasionally; it is ok to deviate, if known to everyone in advance. But if it is unplanned or last-minute change, you may have to compromise with performance, which may not be good for the organization in long run.

Culture to respect lunch and tea break timings for all employees will be helpful in improving working environment and sustainable positive outcome.

Plan B is recipe for failure

Only for life and death kind, or extremely critical situations, one should have plan B. For everything else there should be only Plan A and no other back up plan whatsoever.

It's a normal human tendency which directly or indirectly acts to dilute efforts and seriousness for plan A, since somewhere in the back of mind alternate plan is available in case of failure.

I am sure, you will agree that plan-B is option of second choice and certainly may not deliver output comparable to plan-A. So, why not focus all the energy and resources in making plan-A successful instead of having alternate backup options.

You may think that since there is no plan-B, in case your plan-A fails; you probably lose everything. However, since all your energy is concentrated on execution of only plan-A, chances of success are significantly higher. Alternatively, even if your plan-B succeeds, it will give inferior results as compared to your best plan. On the other hand, over the period of time, the differential positive output from plan-A as compared to plan-B will even compensate for any incidences of failure.

Profile image should represent you 24x7

As a business owner or professional, we have presence on multiple locations in social media. It could be facebook, linkedin, twitter, whatsapp, Instagram, website and many other sites, where profile image is something which acts as our first impression.

You must have noticed that when we meet someone, our body language, facial expressions, attire and behaviour all are observed by other person and result of our meeting depends on all these aspects.

Same impact is created with our profile image which is used on various social networking sites. Profile image is something which interacts with our target audience in our absence 24x7. Profile image can very well be used to create first impression and convey desired message with appropriate use of expressions, background, colour and accessories.

Preferably keep your profile image consistent across all media sites for more effective communication of desired message.

To retain loyal customers, keep a watch on external parameters

As we all know, customer loyalty can be gained by consistently providing good products and services. Businesses take lot of efforts to win loyal customers. But, once acquired, usually these loyal customers are taken for granted.

With current pace of change, easy access to information and increasing aspirations of customers, it is noticed that loyalty can be easily switched for better customer experience and higher perceived value.

To retain loyal customers, we need to keep a continuous watch on our direct and indirect competition, their strategies and unexpressed expectations of customers. This proactive approach will certainly help in retaining loyal customers for longer duration.

Safe vehicle parking can improve Employee's Performance

It may sound strange; but mostly it is observed that employee's performance at work is linked to safe vehicle parking facility.

For most of the people, vehicle is quite important personal asset with emotional attachments. If vehicle is not safely parked and is out of sight for long time; subconsciously, some part of brain is always concerned about the vehicle. Knowingly or unknowing, it affects performance at work.

If safe vehicle parking is provided; it will remove one major distraction for the employee; leading to higher peace of mind and better concentration on work. It will certainly have positive impact on overall performance.

For every vacancy, evaluate both, internal and external options

Vacancy in organization is created by two ways; when someone quits the job or when business need more people for growth.

It is noticed that, first thing comes to mind of the leader is to fill the vacancy from external resource, and recruitment process begins. However, in every such situation, probably best option is to look out for internal talent pool.

It is noticed that, internal talent is ignored many times for filling the vacancy. Sometimes, it could be more effective and cost efficient to give higher responsibility to internal talent by promotion and get external candidate for junior position.

It should not be taken as general rule; but for every such situation equal weightage should be given to internal and external candidates for optimum results in the interest of the organization.

Recertify value proposition at regular interval

Since someone is buying your product or service; it can be safely assumed that they are getting some value. Although in some cases, it may be purely out of need or due to non-availability of alternatives.

With time; value proposition, especially as perceived by the customer may change for various reasons. Many times, since business transactions are happening at regular pace, this change in perceived value may get unnoticed by the business. In such situations, customers may switch to other option without even getting noticed in real time.

There can be many reasons for this change in perceived value. It can be competition, availability of alternatives, changing culture and environment, changes in law of land or increased aspirations of customer. Whatever may be the case, if product and services do not address these issues in time, degrowth of business is inevitable.

To address this challenge, it is the best practice to Re-Certify value proposition of each product and service at regular interval. For most businesses, annual recertification may be sufficient; however, some may need more frequent reviews.

Deliver bad news in person and good news in public

It is a human nature that make it easy to remember bad news or negative information as compared to the good news or positive information. Especially, when the bad news is concerned with others, it easily becomes topic for gossip and has potential of extrapolation out of limits. On the contrary, for getting desired impact for some good news, especially concerned with others, it requires additional efforts.

One of major continuing goal of any organization is to retain good people. Communicating bad news in person will save them from possible humiliation by others and communicating good news in public will create possibilities of getting praise or recognition by others.

So, unless there is any specific known and well thought-out agenda in doing otherwise; always communicate bad news in person and good news in public.

Speed of decision is linked to growth

Success and failure are results of your decisions. Every correct decision will take you couple of steps forward and some incorrect decision may push you a step backword.

It is also a proven fact that decisions taken with appropriate due diligence mostly deliver desired results. As an expert in your own business or working area, everyone must have developed a skill to take relatively more number of right decisions.

If speed of decision making is improved, a greater number of decisions can be made in less time. Since, majority of decisions are taking you few steps forwards, it automatically drives growth.

Off course; one need to improve supporting skills required for decision making to enable right decisions in shortest time without compromising any critical parameters to achieve speed.

Higher the speed of decision making, means more decisions in less time; which can easily trigger exponential growth.

Distribute Authority, but not Responsibility

You must have noticed; many times, organizational actions are totally opposite of this, where responsibilities are clearly distributed but authority is either centralized or have multi-dimensional complexities.

If we look at authority and responsibility from a larger perspective; authority can be defined as something for which designated person is authorized to take all relevant decisions; and responsibility can be defined as ownership of outcome of these actions or decisions.

Let's take an example of very common function of Sales. Here, authority of taking sales decision should be delegated with clarity to respective sales team member. But the responsibility of final sales shall be shared with multiple teams including R&D, Accounts, IT, HR and all support functions.

With this; naturally, rewards will be distributed to all responsible functions, while sales team which is authorized to act will be doing the work with whole hearted support from everyone.

Fire 10 employees every year for healthy growth

It is a known fact that many employees change their job during course of their career. Reasons of leaving the job could be different for each organization. But one thing is common; majority of leaving employees are those who are performing well and have good demand in the job market. With every such exit, average standard of employees in the organization goes down.

You must have noticed; highly skilled and competent people enjoy working in the environment where others are also equally competent and where wavelengths match with each other. Every voluntary exit further deteriorates this desired environment.

One effective way to manage this problem is to identify bottom 10% employees with clearly measurable performance parameters and fire them to get replacement with fresh blood having competent skill sets.

With such practice, in addition to maintaining quality standards in the organization, it will create better environment to discourage good people to leave.

Refine strategy from execution point of view

You will agree; any good strategy is good as long as it is executable.

Many times, you must have noticed, great looking strategies miserably fail on the field. Primary reason for this, in most cases is disconnect with ground realities.

To make a great working strategy; it should be developed in two phases. First phase, where without worrying about ground realities, use the visionary approach to prepare the strategy. This will help in avoiding self-created limitations. Once this phase is complete, take it to second phase where evaluate this strategy within available resource situations and fine tune to optimize it.

If required, do couple of iterations of phase-1 and phase-2 to get a final executable strategy.

Systematically allocate funds for Learning and Development

With the competitive environment, to maintain achieved position and to grow; there is no alternate to keep up-to-date with external changes and overall business environment. We all know, regular learning and development is one important way to achieve this.

It is observed that, although we believe in importance of continuous learning and development of self and our team; mostly it is taken on ad hoc basic and we never notice when we lose pace of required learning.

To avoid this, and for best results; it is suggested to systematically allocate funds for learning and development. Although it may vary for each business and it's current stage; it is advisable to allocate 1% of gross receipts or 5% of net profit for spending on learning and development of self and team. And efforts should be taken not to underspend on the available budget.

Avoid gender bias in communication

When we communicate; it is with the expectations that the recipient connects it with self to make it more effective. If the communication is addressed to some specific gender which is different than the recipient, it will lead to potential disconnect.

Let's assume you address your communication to "The Chairman", and the person happens to be a woman; in most cases you will create a disconnect and may not expect equally effective results. So, in this case, if you address it to "The Chairperson" possibility of desired outcome could be better.

Some other common examples where we may lose with gender biased communication are; "Policeman v/s Police Officer", "Salesman v/s Salesperson" and "Fireman v/s Firefighter".

Just with use of gender-neutral language where you are not sure about who the recipient is; can dramatically change the outcome of your communication in your favour.

Avoid using brain, where SOPs are defined

Usually, standard operating procedures are designed and prepared after careful evaluation of resources and use of experience and expertise. It is supposed to be followed as is without any change.

Sometimes, it may happen that a person executing the work, may take a different step based on own judgement or knowledge in real time. Outcome with such deviation can be good or bad depending on various factors. But in most cases long term negative impact is noticed in the form of collapse of systems.

To ensure that systems drive the business in long term; there should not be any intellectual intervention while executing work using pre-defined SOPs. With time or with expert intervention, SOPs may need to be changed; but all such changes should be evaluated separately and documented to change the SOP for everyone, instead of making random non-documented changes.

We should use brain while preparing the SOPs, but not while implementing it for consistent and best outcome.

Wealth distribution amongst stakeholders should be dynamic

Primarily in partnership firms and family owned businesses; shareholding pattern is decided while starting the business and mostly it continues for long term. Sometimes stakes are further distributed based on legal inheritance.

Individual stakeholder's interest in the business may change over the period of time for various personal or professional reasons. Also newly inducted member with inheritance, may contribute more or less as compared to previous stakeholder. Over the period, all such changes are visible enough to create dissatisfaction for performing member.

For sustained growth of the business, and to ensure that expert brains are retained in full capacity for longer tenure; ownership and wealth distribution should be linked to individual contributions and visible future potential.

For best results and to implement it more effectively, it should be documented in the business charter and should be reviewed at least once in 3 years.

Identify if you are selling painkiller or vitamin

At times; when needed, doctor prescribes us to take painkillers or vitamins. Although we trust the doctor; there is relatively higher reluctance to take vitamins as compared to painkillers. This is probably because we consider painkiller as a need and perceive vitamins as desired or can be avoided category.

In business too, we offer different products or services to our client or customers. Let's define, whether our products or services fall into the category of painkiller or vitamins from customer's point of view.

Different types of efforts are required to promote or sell painkillers and vitamins. Once we know exactly what we are offering, it will help in designing business and marketing strategies to effectively reach the target audience and get better realization.

Chant something in the morning for fluency in conversation

Have you tried eating ice-cream and then talking on some important subject? You must have noticed some change in pronunciation and fluency in speech. Our tongue experiences the same effect every morning after long rest in night. It may be little to be noticed by self, but it is subconsciously noticed by others for sure.

To overcome this challenge every morning, you can start practicing chanting something of your choice which gives sufficient exercise to the muscles required for speech. It can be some slokas in Sanskrit language, or some prayer, or some tongue twisters as you like.

If you practice this every morning before going to work, it will certainly help in getting desired results out of your communication.

Give memorable farewell to employees

We all want employees to stay with us forever; but we know that employees do leave the job at times. And after the exit date; we do not have any control on what image of the organization they project in outside world.

Mostly, organizations ignore or give less importance to employees once the exit is on cards. For any employee, there are many positive and negative memories during the tenure of employment. Overall process of exit decides which memories will be carried and which are erased.

If the exit is not for integrity issues; it is advisable to make the exit experience as memorable as possible for leaving employees; since that will be the last chance for the organization to make an impact.

The farewell experience should make them feel that they should not have left the job. If they carry this feeling of regret to their next job; they will be your brand ambassadors for the lifetime.

Share your dreams to quickly bring these to reality

We all have some dreams for our future. And we do take efforts to fulfil these dreams.

You must have realized; in most cases we need help from the entire universe to fulfil our dreams. Although basic human nature is to help others; but how can someone help you unless they know what you need.

If you share your dreams with your friends, family and entire network; actively or subconsciously large number of people will be working on giving you something which can take you one step closer to your dream.

Additionally, your own conscious efforts will also increase due to pressure created with declaration of dreams in public domain.

Let's be vocal for your dreams, and experience these in reality sooner than later.

Do regular health check-up of your business

As you know; most of the critical illnesses, if detected at early stage, are easy to cure, and cause minimum damage. However, in most cases at early stage, symptoms are not visible or too small to get noticed.

It is applicable to business as well. There can be many challenges in various areas like finance, quality, customer experience, service, employee, vendor and competition. All these challenges start small to get noticed. And when you see the effect, the problems might have become too big to solve and can cause major damage to the business.

Same as diagnostic tests for our body; if business health check-ups are done at regular interval, it will help in addressing issues when these are small or at early stage.

Some of the tools to get business health check-up are external expert interventions, employee engagement analysis, internal audit, customer feedback, competition analysis and many more specific to your business activities.

For healthy growth of the business, regular health check-ups are must.

Always give an offer which you will happily accept

While managing business and personal life; one most important part is negotiation. Whether it is a business deal, sale or purchase transactions, or dealing with employees and associates, you are involved in giving and receiving offers as part of the process.

It's a normal human tendency that when we want to sell or give something, we expect the maximum possible price or value. And when we want to buy or take something, we expect to offer minimum possible price or value. As a result; many times, the deal is either not materialized or fail to create a long-lasting relationship; which is not desirable for any business in long run.

To avoid this, and to get most out of the transaction in long run; try to visualize the situation or deal from other person's point of view and see if you will happily accept your own offer. If your answer is Yes, be assured of success. But, if answer is No, then try to refine your offer.

If you practice this approach; not only your success rate will increase, but it will be sustainable.

Choose to take Good Profit vs Bad Profit

You do make profit in business; but do you know if your profit is Good or Bad? Whenever a customer feels misled, mistreated, coerced, or ignored, you are making Bad Profit. And if a customer is delighted and willing to come back for more, and tell friends and colleagues to do business with the company, you are making Good Profit.

One example can be a mobile operator charging per minute; so, if you speak for 1 minute and 1 second, you will be billed for 2 minutes. Some other operator may be charging per second. In first case, you can call it Bad Profit.

Bad Profit might be higher in the short-term but only Good Profit can drive higher customer lifetime value and sustainability. Companies which take Bad Profit will find it difficult to grow or struggle for survival or ultimately collapse in long run.

When you treat customers like people and not like currency signs, they will respond with positive feedback and loyalty to your brand. If you are interested in long-term good health of your business, taking Good Profit is always better than engaging in Bad Profit.

Ask right question; it will decide what you get

Everyone likes to hear "Yes" in any conversation, which many times does not happen. However, we can definitely increase percentage of "Yes" as an answer in any conversation.

In most cases, whether you will get "Yes" or "No" reply to your question or request, depends on how the request or question is framed.

Sharing one story to explain. Two friends Narendra and Rahul, both chain smokers went to a Temple and wanted permission to smoke from the priest. First, Rahul tried and asked the priest, "Can I smoke while I pray?", as you can guess the answer was strict "No". Now, Narendra tried and asked the priest, "Can I pray while I am smoking?", and off course the answer was "Yes".

You can imagine many such situations in our day-to-day life, where results can be transformed in our favour, just by asking the right question.